No part of this book may be reproduced in any form without written
permission from the publisher. Contact Golden Gate National Parks
Conservancy, Bldg. 201 Fort Mason, San Francisco, CA 94123.

Library of Congress Control Number 2008920019

ISBN 978-1-932519-02-0 Muir Woods Forest Meditations Edition
ISBN 978-1-932519-03-7 Forest Meditations Edition

Photographs: Stephen Joseph
Project and Art Direction: Robert Lieber
Design: Vivian Young
"The Forest Primeval": Michael Hsu
Production: Sarah Lau
National Park Service Advisor: Mia Monroe

Photographs in this book were taken at Muir Woods National Monument,
a primeval forest in Northern California.
Developed and designed in US. Printed in Hong Kong.

GOLDEN GATE NATIONAL PARKS CONSERVANCY
The Parks Conservancy is the nonprofit membership organization created
to preserve the Golden Gate National Parks, enhance the experiences of
park visitors, and build a community dedicated to conserving the parks for
the future. Visit *www.parksconservancy.org*.

FOREST MEDITATIONS

Photographs by Stephen Joseph

Compiled and Edited by Robert Lieber

GOLDEN GATE NATIONAL PARKS CONSERVANCY

THE FOREST PRIMEVAL

There is a place that speaks persistently to memory. It's a place where the secrets of time go to slumber, and the human spirit goes to revive.

In an old-growth forest, we feel closer to the mysteries of the world. We draw strength from the ancient trees and inspiration from their soaring heights. We find peace in the whisper of running water over rock, magic in the dew on a petal, and courage from the slug's slow, stubborn crawl ever onward. So you return often to the forest—to sense again wet leaves beneath your feet and familiar mosses at your fingers.

But unlike the river otter or rhododendron, we cannot live our days under leaves and needles of green and gold. *Forest Meditations* presents a way to the woods, on the days when the hiking boots must stay in your closet. Through a perfect balance of stunning photography by Stephen Joseph and wise words from writers, artists, and sages, we can keep in our memory the quiet beauty of the forest primeval.

So take this book with you. Carry its stories in your heart. And live by its lessons—fully and brightly.

The voice of nature is
always encouraging.

HENRY DAVID THOREAU

It is not so much for its beauty
that the forest makes a claim upon
men's hearts,
as for that subtle something,
that quality of air that emanates
from old trees,
that so wonderfully changes
and renews a weary spirit.

ROBERT LOUIS STEVENSON

In every walk with Nature,
   one receives far more
than [one] seeks.

JOHN MUIR

Trees are the earth's endless effort
to speak to the listening heaven.

RABINDRANATH TAGORE

Everybody needs beauty
as well as bread...
where nature may heal and
give strength to body and soul.

JOHN MUIR

There is something infinitely
    healing in the repeated refrain
    of nature—
the assurance that
    dawn comes after night,
    and spring after the winter.

RACHEL CARSON

For in the true nature of things,
         if we rightly consider,
every green tree is far more glorious
         than if it were made of gold and silver.

MARTIN LUTHER KING

Each of us needs to withdraw from the cares
        which will not withdraw from us.
We need hours of aimless wandering...
        observing the mysterious world of ants
and the canopy of treetops.

MAYA ANGELOU

Those who contemplate the beauty of the earth
find reserves of strength that will
endure as long as life lasts.

RACHEL CARSON

Among the scenes which are deeply
impressed on my mind,
none exceed in sublimity the
primeval forests undefaced by
the hand of man...
no one can stand in these solitudes
unmoved, and not feel that there is
more in man than the mere breath
of his body.

CHARLES DARWIN

Nature does not hurry,
yet everything
is accomplished.

LAO TZU

And this, our life,
        exempt from public haunt,
finds tongues in trees,
books in the running brooks,
sermons in stones,
        and good in everything.

WILLIAM SHAKESPEARE

I do not understand how anyone
can live without some
small place of enchantment
to turn to.

MARJORIE KINNAN RAWLINGS

Walk the Sequoia woods
at any time of the year
and you will say
they are the most
beautiful
and majestic on earth.

JOHN MUIR

Come to the woods, for here is rest.
There is no repose like that of the
green deep woods...

JOHN MUIR

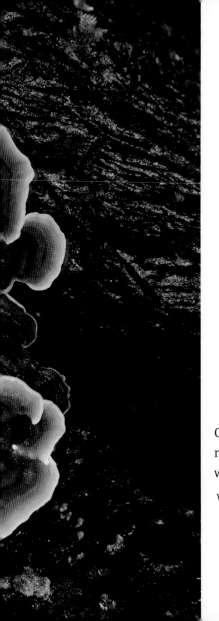

One touch of nature
makes the
whole world kin.

WILLIAM SHAKESPEARE

Wilderness helps us preserve our capacity
for wonder,
    the power to feel, if not to see,
    the miracles of life, of beauty,
    and of harmony around us.

WILLIAM O. DOUGLAS

We can never have enough
of nature.

HENRY DAVID THOREAU

Here man is no longer the center of the world,
only a witness, but a witness who is also
a partner in the silent life of nature,
bound by secret affinities to the trees.

DAG HAMMARSKJÖLD

There are more things
in heaven and earth, Horatio,
than are dreamt of
in your philosophy.

WILLIAM SHAKESPEARE

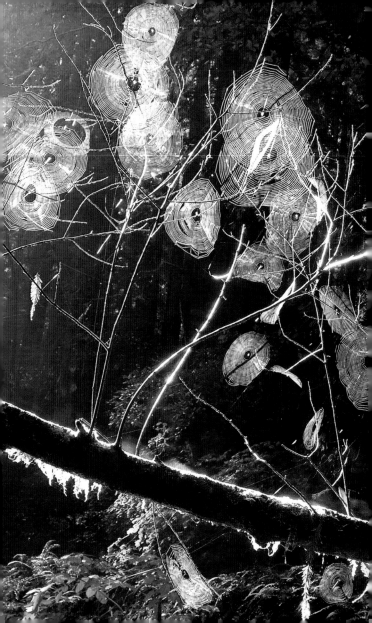

In all things of nature
there is something of the marvelous.

ARISTOTLE

In Wildness lies the hope of the world.

JOHN MUIR

This grand show is eternal.
    It is always sunrise
    somewhere;
the dew is never all dried at once;
    a shower is forever falling;
    vapor is ever rising.

Eternal sunrise,
    eternal sunset, eternal dawn
and gloaming, on sea
    and continents and islands,
    each in its turn,
    as the round earth rolls.

JOHN MUIR

People from a planet
    without flowers would
think we must be mad
    with joy the whole time
to have such things about us.

IRIS MURDOCH

I only went out for a walk,
    and finally concluded to stay out till sundown,
    for going out, I found, was really going in.

JOHN MUIR

Study nature,
love nature,
stay close to nature.
It will never fail you.

FRANK LLOYD WRIGHT

Climb the mountains and get their good tidings.
Nature's peace will flow into you
    as sunshine flows into trees.
The winds will blow their freshness into you,
    and the storms their energy,
while cares will drop off like autumn leaves.

JOHN MUIR

One can never study nature
too much and too hard.

VINCENT VAN GOGH

But to the eyes of the man of imagination, nature is imagination itself.

WILLIAM BLAKE

And I firmly believe that
nature brings solace in all troubles.

ANNE FRANK

The joy of looking and comprehending is nature's most beautiful gift.

ALBERT EINSTEIN

The clearest way into
the Universe
is through
a forest wilderness.

JOHN MUIR

The national park idea, the best idea we ever had,
was inevitable as soon as Americans
learned to confront the wild continent
not with fear and cupidity
but with delight, wonder, and awe.

WALLACE STEGNER

STEPHEN JOSEPH

An environmental landscape photographer with over 40 years of experience, Stephen Joseph has worked with many Bay Area land trust organizations and exhibited his work at the San Francisco Legion of Honor, Oakland Museum, and Ansel Adams Gallery.

Joseph was named Muir Woods Centennial Photographer on the occasion of the woods' 100th anniversary as a National Monument in 2008. Joseph's photography style continued to evolve through his work on the Muir Woods Centennial project. Using digital technology, he created panoramic photographs by splicing several photos of an object or vista together to create one stunning visual representation of his subjects.

"Each photograph of the redwoods often started with as many as 83 photos," Joseph said. "For each tree I photograph, I take several photos of the canopy, the middle of the tree, and its base, and then select the top nine or 12 photos before creating one perfect photo. This kind of photography would not have been possible earlier, as it is today with computer technology— and a lot of fine, digital stitching."

"Capturing the magic of Muir Woods was a challenging but satisfying project for me," Joseph said. "I've always

been interested in history and that is what drew me to this project. I've been creating timeless images of the redwoods by photographing trees during different times of the day and year. My images show the trees with water dripping during early morning hours, and capturing the first burst of light from the sun reflected off the tall base of the trees. All of them— individually and together—work to create a sense of belonging and history for visitors, and that is what I wanted to achieve."

Over the last five years, Joseph has also been collaborating with John Muir historian Bonnie Gisel on a number of projects, including the recently published *Nature's Beloved Son: Rediscovering John Muir's Botanical Legacy*, produced by Heyday publishers, that includes Joseph's exquisite documentation of the plants Muir collected on his travels. A beautiful line of products featuring Joseph's work, including his Muir Woods and John Muir botanical images, are available at *www.parksconservancy.org*. Galleries of Joseph's photography can be found at *www.stephenjosephphoto.com*.

When my son runs down the hill
through the trees, shouting for mama
and laughing as freely as only a baby can,
I cup my hands in stubborn hopefulness,
making him the promise...
I will make this place safe for him,
bring him back to this landscape
throughout his life, this wild country of
beauty and hope and mystery.

DOROTHY ALLISON